CUP or BOWL?

favorite soups from the zingerman's bakehouse kitchen

Amy Emberling

Lindsay-Jean Hard

Lee Vedder

table of contents

5 o'clock cheddar ale
with vegetable broth
16

beef & guinness stew
19

cool as a cucumber
22

creamy quahog chowda
with clam stock
23

heirloom gazpacho
28

fired up fennel & bean
26

kickin' butternut
30

molinaro's mushroom
barley with Parmesan
mushroom broth
32

moroccan harira
36

persian chicken stew
with chicken stock
38

Sri Lankan Lentil
42

tomato de-Vine
44

turkey urfa chili
46

vichyssoise
48

west african
Peanut stew
50

introduction

zingerman's bakehouse 2001: Soup's On!

WHEN WE OPENED the bakery in 1992, having a retail shop was not even an idea in the back of our minds. We were focused on baking a handful of breads and honestly couldn't imagine having the mental capacity to create and manage a shop. We also didn't believe that anyone would make the trip to our nondescript building buried in an industrial park at the edge of Ann Arbor. And besides, Zingerman's Deli was our face to the public and the folks there were doing a fantastic job.

In our myopic focus on executing our craft, we completely missed that there were many other people in the other identical buildings surrounding us who were hungry during the day and were enjoying the aromas of our baking. They let us know! They knocked on the windows and walked in the front door and asked if they could buy some bread. We were surprised, elated, and happy to help them. The development of the shop was then a slow and deliberate process. In 1993, we started selling a few loaves of bread and some "extra" pastries from a card table in the bread bakery. Then we graduated to bookshelves! We started with a cash box and then a portable cash register from an office supply store. By 1996, the flow of customers was significant enough that it warranted building a real shop in the adjacent space. With a dedicated space, we needed to decide who we were and what we wanted to do.

Our vision for the shop has always been to keep it simple and to keep the offerings limited to our baked goods, items related to baking, and good accompaniments to baked foods. Sometime in the late '90s, we began to sell modest pre-made sandwiches for our park neighbors. They were an appealing way to give service to our neighbors and to introduce people to breads they had never tasted. By 2001, we had a buzzing little shop and our guests wanted more variety.

We were challenged to satisfy our guests but stick to our vision. Frank Carollo, Bakehouse Managing Partner, came up with the idea of serving a couple of hot soups every day. Why? Because soup and bread are a natural pair. It made sense. We'd serve soup and give guests a piece of bread to enjoy with it. All these years later, the tradition has continued.

To bring the idea to life, we thought of Mary Kalinowski. Mary had been one of the early members of our baking team. She had personally baked thousands of loaves of bread with us before she left to open a soup restaurant in her hometown of Hamtramck, MI. Frank invited Mary to come and make soup with us. Fortunately, she agreed and we were off. Mary's creations include Tomato De-Vine, our Wednesday standard, Turkey Urfa Chile, our Thursday standard, and West African Peanut Stew. Mary stayed with us for years and we are grateful for the soup legacy she left with us.

So, many years later, our soup repertoire has grown tremendously. We rotate the menu seasonally, make enough to sell some cold, and even teach some of the recipes at BAKE!, our hands-on baking school. Finally, we decided to share some of the recipes with you in this little book. Grab a chunk of bread and dive in! Soup's on!

—AMY EMBERLING, MANAGING PARTNER

a history of soup
some culinary tidbits to whet the appetite

It is impossible to think of any good meal, no matter how plain or elegant, without soup or bread in it.

—M.F.K. FISHER, THE PREEMINENT AMERICAN FOOD WRITER, 1978

CHOCK FULL of flavorful ingredients, simmered and seasoned with a rich array of herbs and spices, the soups we make here at the Bakehouse reflect a cornucopia of culinary influences and history from across the globe. Our recipes are rooted in soup traditions that hail from not only here at home but also those way beyond our American shores—from the British Isles, France, and Spain to the Mediterranean and Middle East, from Morocco and West Africa to South Asia. Soup, one of the world's first prepared dishes, is universal and infinitely adaptable to the diet, change of seasons, and the local flora, fauna, and terroir found in any given culture. Throughout history and around the world, soup has brought hearty sustenance, warmth, and good health to people from every walk of life, becoming, along with its whole-grain counterpart, porridge, the unpretentious, everyday comfort food for all of civilization.

Soup in the beginning

Soup is said to be as old as the history of cooking and as ancient as the devising of vessels to hold and boil liquid. Archeologists believe we've been making soup for at least 20,000 years! That's some history! Indeed, soup has been at the forefront of our gastronomic evolution ever since our ancient Neolithic forebears advanced from "simply eating wild grains, seeds, or meat placed in or near a fire, to preparing rudimentary dishes that followed some vague notion of food as a pleasing experience rather than the simple necessity of fueling the body," so notes culinary historian Victoria R. Rumble, author of the ground-breaking book, *Soup Through the Ages* (2009). Animal hides, placed over a fire or heated with hot stones were the first soup pots, followed by earthen or metal cauldrons, into which our ancient ancestors added whatever ingredients could be foraged, harvested, or killed, developing amazing one-pot wonders that remain to this day in a perpetual state of evolution.

Through the millennia, the long cooking of soup, boiled over a fire or by hot stones, proved a simple and effective way to draw nourishment and flavor from the meagerest quantities of meat, fish, vegetables, roots, grains, legumes, nuts, and herbs. Submerging these foods in boiling water, versus roasting them over an open fire, allowed them to cook faster and thoroughly, catching all their released juices and starches into a flavorful, nourishing broth. Soup, thus prepared, and in such combinations of ingredients, was pivotal in expanding the diet of our ancient ancestors, allowing them to eat a broader variety of food.

Soup's early evolution as a culinary staple

After those first Stone-Age catch-as-catch-can soups of wild plants and animals that nomadic hunter gatherers improvised, and after the agricultural triumphs of the Neolithic Revolution, which saw vast fields of grain and pulses (legumes) spring up in the Fertile Crescent, Asia, and Europe, ushering in early civilization, it was the cooking of grains and pulses in a water-based broth that brought soup to the proverbial culinary table. These were the stuff of early soups, when cooking grains and pulses in boiling water caused them to release their starchy arsenal of nutrition and flavor into the broth, making the soup thick, filling, and nourishing, not to mention tasty!

how soup got its name

Soup's etymology reveals much about the dish's culinary evolution, with its quintessential pairing with bread, especially as it unfolded in continental Europe. What we now call "soup" has had a variety of names over the course of its long history. The nomenclature begins with "gruel," a cereal-based dish in which grains were roasted and ground into a paste and then boiled in water. Its simple constitution and preparation made it accessible to everyone in every culture where grain was grown or available in its wild state.

"Broth" is recorded in Europe from about the year 1000, with medieval recipes alluding to its soup-like character and one-pot method of preparation. By the 15th century, notes food historian, Janet Clarkson, in her book, *Soup: A Global History* (2010), such dishes were known as *potages*, which hails from the French word *potage*, meaning "that which is put in the pot."

In its earliest days, "a *potage* was the one-pot basic meal of every household. It was a thick (if you were lucky) 'mess' of a staple grain or pulse, with the addition (if you were very lucky) of some available greens or other vegetables. If the name and the style of the dish sound suspiciously like *porridge*," Clarkson goes on to explain, "it is because they are essentially the same thing. In fact, according to the Oxford English Dictionary, the word *porridge* is simply a variant of *pottage*." By the 17th century, in England and France, Clarkson continues, *potages* had evolved considerably, becoming "highly complex 'made dishes'—such as an entire chicken surrounded by various other delicacies and garnishes, sitting in a pool of its cooking liquid. The liquid itself was by this time the crucial component, as the definition of *potage* from the 1606 *Tresor de la langue française* indicates: 'It is water boiled in flesh, herbs, and other meat in a cooking pot'."

As *potage* gained ground in the culinary lexicon, so too did the word *sop* (*soupe* in French), referring to pieces of bread used to *sop* up the liquid portion of the dish. *Sop* and *soupe*, in turn, stem from the Latin verb *suppare*, meaning to soak. In the 1606 French dictionary, noted above, *une soupe* was essentially defined as "bread with broth." Sopping had several advantages, notes Clarkson: "it softened up hard or stale bread at the same time it avoided wasting a single delicious drop of the broth . . . In the way that words do, the concept of *sops* extended to give us our English words *sup*, *soup* and *supper*, and was eventually transferred to the liquid part of the dish." So there you have it—how the pairing of soup with bread came to be.

Soup's enduring culinary Legacy

Soup maven extraordinaire, Patricia Solley, in her celebratory book, *An Exaltation of Soups* (2004), based on her prolific website Soupsong.com, summed up soup's culinary history and cultural significance this way:

> *Look at a bowl of soup and see the evolution of foods created in remote locations over thousands and thousands of years, made into recipes passed from hand to hand, transported on the backs of Indian, Asian, and Arab traders, Roman soldiers, and European explorers, all the way to your supermarket.*

> *Eat a bowl of soup and savor mouthfuls of human resolve since Neolithic times to bring warmth, health, and richness into the lives of their family members, their tribe, their community, their culture.*

> *Consider a bowl of soup from any culture, and think how it came to reflect that specific people, their times of celebration, their passages of life, their most intimate life experiences.*

—LEE VEDDER, BAKEHOUSE HISTORIAN

choosing ingredients
a few basic tips

MOST OF THE SOUPS in this cookbook are relatively easy to make—they have straightforward recipes and rarely have lengthy ingredient lists. As is always the case with our food, what distinguishes our versions from someone else's is great execution and the best, most flavorful ingredients we can find. As we say at Zingerman's, "You really can taste the difference."

Below you'll find our recommendations for what to use for the most common ingredients. For ingredients that appear in only one recipe, we will include suggestions on what to buy in the Tip section of the recipe.

butter

We use unsalted butter in all our recipes, whether it's for scones or soups. Salt in butter is unregulated, so depending on the brand you choose, it may be more or less salty. It's easiest to control the salt by using unsalted butter and adding the amount of salt that is optimal for the recipe.

milk & cream

Fat = flavor! Just as we use butter because it's more flavorful than shortening and margarine, you'll notice that our recipes call for full-fat dairy products like heavy cream and whole milk. At the risk of sounding like a broken record, it provides more flavor and you really can taste the difference!

spices

Spices, like practically all foods, come in a full range of quality. For the best spices possible, finding a specialty grocer or spice store in your area could give you the most flavorful choices. Another good option is to purchase spices online, like from long-time Zingerman's partner, Épice de Cru at spicetrekkers.com. The next best choice is to use newly bought spices. Spices lose their aroma and flavor over time so new ones from the store will be much better than the jar in your cupboard that's been open for a year.

marash pepper

This is one spice worthy of its own entry. Marash peppers hail from Turkey and can be used fresh or dried and ground into flakes. The dried flakes are fruity and earthy in flavor and have medium heat. It adds a wonderful complexity to a couple of soups in this collection. It's also great sprinkled on other dishes, like salad and fish, and mixed with oil for dipping bread. It's readily available online through Zingerman's Mail Order and other purveyors.

urfa pepper flakes

These are super flavorful, red-black pepper flakes with a flavor profile that is sweet, earthy, and smoky. To make these pepper flakes, special deep purple peppers are picked, cut, dried in the sun, then wrapped and sweated at night for over a week. During the week, their color changes from purple to burgundy to almost black. They have a moderate level of heat. They add a distinctive flavor to a couple of soups in this cookbooklet, but you can also use them on salad, pasta, or meat.

herbs

For recipes that call for herbs, we almost always call for fresh—you'll get the most flavor. And when the herbs have soft stems, like cilantro and parsley, it's okay to use them along with the leaves, just chop them up finely.

sea salt

In the bakery, we use finely ground sea salt for everything from breads to baked goods to soups. It allows us to avoid the off-flavors of iodized salt and to benefit from the more complex flavors of sea salt, but if you are raring to get cooking and don't have sea salt, go ahead and use whatever salt you have on hand. These soups have so many other flavors going on that you won't taste the difference. Do note though, that different types of salt have different levels of saltiness, so they aren't always a direct substitution.

saltiness

For small amounts (like 1 teaspoon or less), fine sea salt and table salt can be used interchangeably. For larger amounts, follow this guide:

TABLE SALT	FINE SEA SALT	MORTON KOSHER SALT or FLEUR DE SEL	DIAMOND CRYSTAL KOSHER SALT or MALDON SEA SALT
1 tablespoon	1¼ tablespoon	1½ tablespoons	2 tablespoons

stock & broth

We love making our own (and share 4 different recipes for them in this book), but we also understand that sometimes it's more convenient to pick up pre-made stock or broth. Flavors can vary widely by brand, so our suggestion is similar to the standard for cooking with wine—just as it's best to cook with wine that you'd enjoy drinking, it's also best to cook with a stock that you enjoy the flavor of on its own. Different stocks can also have strikingly different levels of salt, so when using pre-made ones, it's especially important to add the prescribed salt to the soup to taste.

Produce

This likely goes without saying (we're going to say it anyway), but we always recommend buying produce when it's in season—that's when it's going to taste its best. For instance, gazpacho season in the Bakeshop is dictated by Michigan's tomato season. We know we'll have it in late summer, but some years it might start a little earlier, others a little later, but the gazpacho always stops when we can no longer get locally grown heirloom tomatoes—it just doesn't taste as good without them. As with other ingredients, use full-flavored produce. It doesn't need to look beautiful but it should taste great.

vinagre de jerez

A couple of our soup recipes call for vinagre de Jerez, or sherry vinegar. This sherry vinegar has its own Denominación de Origen, meaning its production and quality are monitored. For a vinegar to be labeled as vinagre de Jerez, it must be aged in oak for a minimum of 6 months in a particular part of the Spanish province of Cádiz known as the "sherry triangle." All of this is to say, it's an especially flavorful vinegar that's worth seeking out.

equipment
the right tool for the job

digital scale
While this isn't a requirement, it's recommended. We do all of our baking *and* cooking by weight and encourage home cooks to do the same, as it allows for much greater consistency than volume measures. These recipes were created in grams and then rounded to the closest reasonable volume equivalent, which works out just fine, since soups are more forgiving than baked goods.

stockpot
When we say large stockpot, we mean one that comfortably holds one gallon (16 cups) or more, as most of the recipes in this book make about that much soup.

immersion blender
For the soups that are puréed, we call for using an immersion blender—it's the fastest and easiest option and creates fewer dishes to wash! But if you don't have one, a blender or food processor will work, too. If it's a hot soup, let it cool off slightly, only fill the blender about halfway, and cover the lid of the blender with a towel to prevent hot soup splashes. Whether hot or cold, the soup will likely need to be blended in batches.

colander and fine mesh sieve
We use a colander for draining and rinsing canned beans and a fine mesh sieve for straining ingredients out of stock— in the latter case, make sure you have a bowl or pot underneath the fine mesh sieve, so you don't lose the stock you just made!

peeler
You won't use this one very often, so a paring knife would also suffice. Unless we specifically call for an ingredient to be peeled, like the sweet potatoes in the West African Peanut Stew, it doesn't need to be peeled. There's a lot of nutrients and flavor in the outermost layers of produce that we don't want to lose—just wash them well before chopping. (You always do that though, right?!)

preparing to cook
ready...set...Start your stovetops!

WE WANT YOU to be successful when you make these recipes. There's a greater chance you will be if you follow these steps:

1. Read the recipe all the way through before you start to do anything else! Look for:
   a. Ingredients you need. Do you have them? Do you have enough of them?
   b. Steps you need to take prior to starting to cook, such as soaking beans overnight.
   c. Equipment you need.

2. Preheat your oven. (This applies more to baking, but there's at least one soup in here that will require you to turn your oven on!)

3. Measure all of the ingredients you need for the recipe into separate containers. Yes, we mean it! This helps tremendously to make sure that you measure items correctly and don't leave anything out of the recipe or put it in twice.

4. Clear your work area of anything unnecessary for the project. A neat space makes it much easier to cook.

storage
make it last

GENERALLY SPEAKING, many soups keep well in an airtight container in the fridge for 3 to 4 days. Soups can often be frozen for up to 3 months, too—either in large or single-serving containers—making a strong case for cooking up a double batch and setting yourself up for dinner successes down the line. If you're freezing soup, let the soup completely cool down, transfer it into an airtight container, and make sure you leave room in the container for the soup to expand as it freezes—about ½ to 1 inch of space between the soup and the lid should suffice. And then label the container! It's easily identifiable now, but 5 weeks from now, you'll find yourself scratching your head as to whether that frozen block is Turkey Urfa Chili or Moroccan Harira. If you are making soup with the express purpose of freezing it, consider slightly undercooking your vegetables—they'll continue to cook when you reheat the soup and no one likes mushy vegetables.

As is often the case in life and in cooking, there are exceptions to the rule. Dairy-based soups tend to separate once thawed and raw vegetables and pasta don't take kindly to being frozen. (So, don't freeze your Cool as a Cucumber soup, that one's a double whammy of dairy-based and raw vegetables!) Soups that aren't entirely dairy-based, but have dairy in them, like Kickin' Butternut, can be successfully frozen. The best option is to leave the dairy out of the soup as you're making it, freeze the soup, and then add in the dairy when you're ready to enjoy it. It's also okay to freeze it with the dairy in it, just reheat it gently and know that it might separate a little as you do—a few stirs should bring it all back together.

the recipes

5 o'clock cheddar ale
with vegetable stock

This soup has been a Thursday standard in our shop for at least a decade. It's been so long that none of us can remember exactly when we started to make it. Summer or winter, it seems to satisfy. Its distinctive flavor comes from sharp cheddar cheese, vinagre de Jerez, Marash pepper, and a well-chosen amber ale. You'll need one bottle and part of another for the recipe—feel free to enjoy the rest of the second bottle yourself as you cook! (Check out the ingredients section for more on vinagre de Jerez and Marash pepper.)

Serves 6 to 8 as a main dish

Butter	½ cup	112 grams
Yellow onion, ½-inch dice	1 cup	150 grams
Carrot, ½-inch dice	1 cup	150 grams
Celery, ½-inch dice	1¼ cups	150 grams
Garlic, minced	3 cloves	25 grams
Fine sea salt		
Amber ale	1¾ cups	415 grams
Vegetable stock (see recipe that follows)	4 cups	948 grams
Whole milk	4¾ cups	1211 grams
Sharp cheddar, grated	8 cups	867 grams
All-purpose flour	1¼ cups	173 grams
Marash pepper flakes	2½ teaspoons	6 grams
Ground white pepper	¾ teaspoon	2 grams
Vinagre de Jerez (sherry vinegar)	2¼ teaspoons	10 grams

1. Make vegetable stock (see recipe that follows).

2. In a large stockpot over medium heat, melt the butter, then add the onions, carrots, celery, garlic, and a generous sprinkle of salt, and sauté until the vegetables are tender and onions are translucent, 10 to 15 minutes. Be careful not to brown them.

3. Add the beer and simmer for 5 minutes.

4. In a separate pot, bring the vegetable stock to a simmer.

5. Add the flour to the beer and vegetable mixture. Stir and cook until the mixture thickens and starts to stick to the pan. Gradually pour in the milk, stirring as you do, and then bring the soup to a simmer.

6. Add the hot vegetable stock to the soup.

7. Remove the pot from the heat and purée with an immersion blender.

8. Put the puréed soup back onto the stove on medium to low heat, slowly add the grated cheese, stirring constantly to avoid scorching.

9. Turn off the burner and season the soup with vinagre de Jerez, Marash pepper, white pepper, and additional salt if needed.

bread pairing
Consider pairing this one with True North toast soldiers for dunking.

continued on following page >

Simple Vegetable Stock

Makes about 5 cups

Carrot	2 large	186 grams
Yellow onion	1 medium	163 grams
Celery	2 large stalks	140 grams
Bay leaf	1	
Fresh parsley	2 or 3 sprigs	5 grams
Fresh thyme	1 or 2 sprigs	1 gram
Whole black peppercorns	2	

1. Cut all of the vegetables into large pieces. In a medium stockpot, add the vegetables, parsley, thyme, bay leaf, peppercorns, and 6 cups of water. Bring to a boil over medium-high heat, then reduce to medium-low and simmer gently for one hour. Strain the broth through a fine mesh sieve and reserve 4 cups for the soup—any extra can be refrigerated or frozen for later use.

beef & guinness stew

We had a brief flirtation with food from the British Isles and this stew and our Cornish meat pies, called pasties, are the recipes that made it into our regular repertoire. We bring out the Beef & Guinness Stew in the winter when we're ready to eat something deep in flavor and filling. Basic beef stew is generally made with beef stock. The French improve it with red wine, and here the Irish improve it with the rich, malty, sweet and slightly bitter Guinness stout. All of these flavors come through in the final stew. Add smoky bacon and the distinctive taste of fresh rosemary to create a nourishing meal.

Serves 6 to 8 as a main dish

Bacon, thick slice	4 slices	109 grams
All-purpose flour	½ cup	73 grams
Beef stew meat, cubed	1 (3-lb) pkg	
Fine sea salt & ground black pepper		
Canola oil	2 tablespoons	28 grams
Butter	2 tablespoons	28 grams
Yellow onion, ½-inch dice	4 cups	572 grams
Cremini mushrooms, quartered	2 cups	227 grams
Carrots, ½-inch dice	2 cups	299 grams
Celery, ½-inch dice	2 cups	245 grams
Guinness Stout	2 (19-oz) cans	
Beef stock	4 cups	948 grams
Fresh rosemary leaves, minced	2 teaspoons	2 grams
Dried thyme	2 teaspoons	2 grams

continued on following page >

> beef & guinness stew, continued

bread pairing
Our Paesano bread is a perfect accompaniment enjoyed with some Irish Kerrygold butter.

1. In a large stockpot, over medium heat, cook the bacon until crispy. Remove the bacon with tongs and drain on a piece of paper towel. Pour out the bacon fat and save for another use, then wipe out the pan. When the bacon is cool, chop it into small pieces, ¼-inch or smaller.

2. In a small bowl, add the all-purpose flour, cubed beef, and a generous sprinkle of salt and pepper, then mix to combine.

3. In the large stockpot, heat the oil and butter over medium heat until the butter has melted, then add the onions and sauté until tender and translucent, about 10 to 15 minutes.

4. Carefully add the beef in a single layer, and let the beef sear for a few minutes before turning with tongs to cook the other side to create a nice crust on the meat. When both sides are browned, remove and set aside beef pieces, and repeat with any meat that did not fit in the initial layer. When all the beef has been seared, remove all of the onions and meat from the pot and reserve for later.

5. If necessary, add more butter and oil to the stockpot. Add mushrooms and sauté until cooked, about 10 minutes. Remove and set aside with the reserved meat and onions.

6. Add the celery and carrots to the stockpot, along with a sprinkle of salt, and sauté, stirring occasionally until soft, 10 to 15 minutes. Remove vegetables and set aside with the mushrooms, meat, and onions.

7. In the stockpot over high heat, add the Guinness. Let it boil and use a wooden spoon to scrape the browned bits off the bottom of the pot.

8. Return everything to the stockpot—bacon, onions, beef, mushrooms, carrots, and celery and add the beef stock, rosemary, and thyme. Allow the soup to come to a boil, then turn the heat down to medium-low and gently simmer the stew until the beef is fully cooked and very tender, and the stew reduces, 1 to 1½ hours, stirring occasionally.

9. Taste and season as needed with salt and pepper.

scottish baps with beef & guinness stew

At BAKE!, our hands-on baking school, Beef & Guinness Stew takes a star turn in the popular class, *Dinner Series: British Isles*, where students make the rich and flavorful stew from start to finish. For sopping up the stewy sauce, we also teach them to make soft and tasty Scottish Baps, dreamy little dinner rolls that pair beautifully with the stew, so much so, we're including our BAKE! recipe here for you to make at home.

Makes 8 rolls

Milk (whole, room temp)	¾ cup	171 grams
Water (room temp)	2 tablespoons	27 grams
Butter (82% milk fat, room temp)	3 tablespoons	41 grams
Honey	1 tablespoon	18 grams
Instant yeast	1 teaspoon	
All-purpose flour	2 cups + 2 teaspoons	291 grams
Sea salt	¾ teaspoon	

1. Preheat a conventional oven to 400°, 20 minutes before baking.

2. In a mixing bowl combine the milk, water, butter, honey, instant yeast, and ½ of the flour. Stir until mixture looks like thick pancake batter. Add the rest of the flour and the sea salt. Stir to combine.

3. Scrape the dough onto your work surface and knead, by hand, for 6 to 8 minutes. The dough will be sticky. Once kneaded, spray the bowl with nonstick cooking spray, place dough back into the bowl and cover with plastic. Ferment dough at room temperature for 1 hour.

4. Scrape dough onto a floured work surface, divide it into 8 equal size pieces and shape each one into a ball. Flour the tops of the balls and let them sit, covered in plastic, for 10 minutes.

5. After 10 minutes, flatten the balls with your hand and then, with a rolling pin, roll each one into a 4-inch oval. Flour the tops of the ovals and using your thumb, press hard into the middle of each one, leaving an impression in the dough.

6. Place the ovals onto a parchment-lined baking sheet and cover with plastic. Let them rest for 30–45 minutes, until nearly doubled in size.

7. Once ready, sift flour over the Baps and press the centers again with your thumb.

8. Bake the Baps for 8 to 10 minutes or until light golden brown. Cool for 5 minutes before eating. Store any leftovers in a plastic bag. Baps can be frozen.

cool as a cucumber

bread pairing
We like to serve this soup with Dill Pogácsa.

This chilled soup is both refreshing and rich at the same time. Not only will it help you beat the heat, but it also helps fight food waste at the same time. We've been looking at so-called scraps with fresh eyes, and have stopped peeling a number of items at the Bakehouse as a result. Carrots, apples, and bananas all keep their peels on for carrot cakes, apple pies, and banana breads, which led us to test this soup without peeling the cucumbers first, as we'd always done. It turned out the soup was just as delicious, and now, more nutritious as well—so keep your peeler in the drawer.

Serves 6 to 8 as a main dish

English cucumbers, seeded and roughly chopped	3½	1021 grams
Vinagre de Jerez (sherry vinegar)	¼ cup	41 grams
Sour cream	1¾ cups	397 grams
Fresh dill leaves, loosely packed, then finely chopped	¾ cup	18 grams
Fine sea salt	2 teaspoons	12 grams
Ground black pepper	2 teaspoons	5 grams
Heavy cream	¾ cup	184 grams
English cucumber, seeded and ¼-inch dice	1	170 grams
Scallions, white and green parts thinly sliced	½ bunch	41 grams

1. In a large food processor, purée the roughly chopped cucumber and vinegar until smooth, then transfer to a large bowl.

2. Whisk in the sour cream, heavy cream, dill, salt, and pepper until just combined.

3. Stir in the diced cucumber and scallions.

4. Cover the bowl with a lid or plastic wrap and refrigerate soup until well chilled, at least a few hours, but ideally overnight.

creamy quahog chowda
with clam stock

In his youth, Frank Carollo worked at what was then a popular Ann Arbor restaurant called Maudes. From what he's told us, they made gallons upon gallons of soup. Frank is a skilled storyteller so we're not entirely sure about the authenticity of his description. Regardless, one of Frank's favorite soups was Clam Chowder. We decided to make one ourselves. Frank chose Quahog clams, an East Coast variety, perhaps reminding him of Maine, one of his preferred places to visit. The briny smell of the clam stock will transport you to the ocean.

Serves 6 to 8 as a main dish

Butter, divided	6 tablespoons	84 grams
Yellow onion, ½-inch dice	1½ cups	227 grams
Celery, ½-inch dice	1¾ cups	227 grams
Fresh thyme leaves	1 tablespoon	2 grams
Bay leaf	1	
Fine sea salt		
Garlic, minced	3 cloves	25 grams
Clam stock (see recipe that follows)	10 cups	2370 grams
Red Bliss potatoes	1 lb	
All-purpose flour	⅓ cup	48 grams
Half & half	1½ cups	356 grams
Fresh clam meat (from clam stock)	¾ cup	170 grams
Canned clam meat	1 (6.5-oz) can	
Ground white pepper	1 teaspoon	2 grams
Parsley, finely chopped	¼ cup	5 grams

continued on following page >

1. Make clam stock (see recipe that follows), reserving the fresh clam meat for the chowder, chopping it into small bite-size pieces.

2. In a large stockpot over medium heat, melt 2 tablespoons butter and add the onion, celery, thyme, and bay leaves and sauté until the vegetables are tender and translucent, 10 to 15 minutes.

3. Add garlic and cook until fragrant, an additional 1 to 2 minutes, taking care not to let it brown.

4. Add clam stock and potatoes and bring to a simmer, cooking the potatoes almost tender, 10 to 15 minutes.

5. While potatoes are cooking, make a butter and flour roux: in a separate saucepan over medium-high heat, melt 4 tablespoons butter and whisk in flour until smooth. While continuing to whisk, allow roux to cook and bubble for at least 1 minute. Do not brown the roux.

6. Once potatoes are cooked, add roux to chowder and continue to simmer, stirring occasionally, until thickened, 10 to 15 minutes.

7. Once chowder is thickened, add the half & half and fresh and canned chopped clams and bring chowder to proper serving temperature, over low heat, but do not boil to prevent scorching.

8. Add white pepper and parsley and season to taste with additional salt.

bread pairing
This soup pairs well with thick slices of toasted and buttered Bakehouse White.

Clam Stock

Makes about 10 cups

Fresh whole cherrystone quahog clams	8 lbs	
Yellow onion, roughly chopped	1 large	470 grams
Celery, roughly chopped	3 large stalks	210 grams
Fresh thyme	8 to 10 sprigs	5 grams
Fresh parsley	2 or 3 sprigs	5 grams
Bay leaves	2	

1. Tap each clam to make sure they are sealed tight. Sealed clams are alive. Rinse each clam with cold water and scrub off any sand or grit.

2. Place all of the ingredients in a large stockpot. Fill the pot with cold water up to 3 inches from the brim.

3. Bring to a boil, then immediately turn off the heat and allow the stock to steep for 10 minutes.

4. Remove the pot from heat and, using tongs, remove clams from the stock.

5. Strain the stock and measure out 8 cups for the chowder. If you have extra stock it can be frozen and used in a risotto or pasta sauce.

6. Remove clam meat from the shells and chop into small bite-sizes pieces for the chowder.

fired up fennel & bean

There's nothing bland about this bean soup! The combination of garlic, red pepper flakes, caramelized onions and fennel are sure to fire up your tastebuds.

We're crazy about the Roncadella Parmigiano-Reggiano we use in our Parmesan Pepper bread, so we always save the rinds to add complexity to our soups. Try this yourself. It's easy to stockpile rinds in the freezer and pull them out to add a big dose of flavor to any soup. Don't have rinds? Substitute vegetable stock and grate some parmesan onto each bowl for a flavorful garnish. If you leave it out entirely, this soup becomes a tasty vegan option.

Serves 6 to 8 as a main dish

Olive oil	3 tablespoons	45 grams
Fennel bulbs, cored and thinly sliced	3 medium	757 grams
Yellow onion, ½-inch dice	4 cups	603 grams
Fine sea salt		
Minced garlic	¼ cup	60 grams
Crushed red pepper flakes	4 teaspoons	9 grams
Parmesan rinds	1½ cups	363 grams
Cannellini beans, drained & rinsed	4 (15.5-oz cans)	
Fresh basil leaves	1½ cups	136 grams

tip!

If you don't have a scale, it can be hard to measure Parmesan rinds. Aim for four large pieces, each about 4-by-4 inches.

bread pairing

This soup is particularly good with our Focaccia.

1. In a large stockpot, heat the oil over medium heat until shimmering, then add the onion, fennel, and a generous sprinkle of salt, and sauté until the vegetables are caramelized, 45 to 60 minutes, stirring occasionally. Aim for a warm, rich, brown color—the longer you let the vegetables caramelize, the more flavorful they'll be.

2. Add the garlic and red pepper flakes and sauté until fragrant, about 1 minute, taking care not to brown the garlic.

3. Add 15 cups of water and Parmesan rinds, bring to a boil over medium-high heat, then reduce to medium-low and let simmer with the lid on until the Parmesan rinds become soft, at least one hour. Remove and discard rinds.

4. Add the beans to soup, cook until heated through, about 10 minutes, then salt to taste.

5. Chiffonade the basil (see tip below), then stir it in.

tip!

Chiffonade is a term to describe cutting leafy greens, like basil or spinach, into thin strips. Simply stack the leaves on top of each other, tightly roll them up, and then thinly slice the rolled-up bundle.

heirloom gazpacho

Save this classic chilled soup for hot August days when tomatoes are at their peak—look for locally grown heirlooms of any variety and you can't go wrong. The version we sell is vegan, but if you don't need it to be, consider adding a little anchovy paste—we love the umami component it adds to the soup.

Serves 6 to 8 as a main dish

Heirloom tomatoes, roughly chopped	3 medium-large	1361 grams
Yellow onion, roughly chopped	½ large	194 grams
Red bell pepper, roughly chopped	½ large	65 grams
Green bell pepper, roughly chopped	½ large	65 grams
Garlic, peeled and halved	2 or 3 cloves	19 grams
Basil leaves, loosely packed	1½ cups	26 grams
English cucumber, seeded, ¼-inch dice	1	434 grams
Vinagre de Jerez (sherry vinegar)	⅓ cup	81 grams
Extra virgin olive oil	3 tablespoons	38 grams
Lime zest	from 1 lime	
Lime juice	¼ cup	35 grams
Urfa pepper flakes	2 teaspoons	6 grams
Fine sea salt		
Anchovy paste (optional)	1 teaspoon	5 grams

bread pairing

Serve this summer staple with grilled slices of Green Olive Paesano.

1. In a full-size food processor (11+ cup capacity) fitted with blade attachment, pulse tomatoes until they resemble a chunky salsa (5 to 7 pulses).

2. Add onion, peppers, garlic, and basil to the food processor, pulse until finely chopped (8 to 9 pulses), and pour the mixture into a large bowl.

3. Stir in the cucumbers, vinegar, olive oil, lime zest and juice, pepper flakes, a generous sprinkle of sea salt, and the anchovy paste, if using.

4. Cover the bowl and refrigerate until chilled and the flavors have had a chance to meld, several hours or overnight.

gazpacho's spanish heritage

Drawing from the culinary traditions of Arab and Roman culture, and the introduction of New World ingredients, traditional gazpacho hails from the province of Andalusia in southern Spain, a centuries-old farming region noted for its vineyards, wheat fields, and cork trees, as well as its olive, almond, and citrus groves. Originally, the cold soup was sustenance for Andalusian field workers, who were given a food ration of bread and oil. The stale bread with added garlic, almonds, olive oil, vinegar, salt, and any available vegetables, pounded in a mortar with added water, made for a thirst-quenching soup in the blazing summer heat, and was easily assimilated to nourish the body. With the introduction of the tomato and cucumber from the New World and Asia respectively, during the Age of Exploration (1400–1600), gazpacho evolved into a decidedly Spanish dish. The presence of the Moors in Spain until 1492 also influenced the soup's distinctive character. Etymologists believe the word "gazpacho" stems from the Mozarabic (Spanish Christians living under Moorish rule) word *caspa* meaning "fragments," referencing the small pieces of bread, which were ripped up and served with the traditional Andalusian soup, as well as the chopped vegetables, nuts, and aromatics that formed its base.

kickin' butternut

This creamy squash soup is a fall favorite among our regular customers—they start asking for it in late summer, already eagerly anticipating the change of seasons. Its kicky flavor comes from a combination of chipotles in adobo sauce, fresh cilantro, and smoked cumin. We love the flavor that smoked cumin lends to this soup, but if you can't find it, regular ground cumin will be just fine.

Serves 6 to 8 as a main dish

Butternut squash	2 medium	1814 grams
Butter	9 tablespoons	130 grams
Yellow onion, ½-inch dice	1⅓ cups	202 grams
Celery, ½-inch dice	1½ cups	202 grams
Carrots, ½-inch dice	1⅓ cups	202 grams
Fine sea salt & ground black pepper		
Vegetable stock	5 cups	1185 grams
Chipotle peppers in adobo sauce	Scant ¼ cup	50 grams
Ground smoked cumin	1½ teaspoons	3 grams
Heavy cream	1⅔ cups	389 grams
Cilantro, leaves finely chopped	1 bunch	86 grams

bread pairing

Pair this one with a hearty slice of Farm bread or a piece of crusty French Baguette.

1. Preheat the oven to 375°F.

2. Cut the butternut squash in half, leaving the skin on, and scoop out the stringy interior and seeds. Discard the squash guts or save the seeds for roasting. Place squash halves on a baking sheet and roast skin-side up in the oven until fork-tender, about an hour. To minimize sticking, squash can be lightly oiled with a neutral-flavored oil or placed on parchment paper. Allow the cooked squash to cool enough to comfortably handle.

3. While the squash is cooling, in a large stockpot, melt the butter over medium heat, add the onion, celery, carrots, and a generous sprinkle of salt and pepper, and sauté until soft, 10 to 15 minutes.

4. Scoop out the squash flesh, adding it to the stockpot and discarding the skins. Add vegetable broth to the stockpot until the top of the vegetables are just covered in liquid. Any additional broth can be reserved for another use.

5. Bring the soup to a boil over medium-high heat, then reduce heat to medium-low and let simmer with the lid on for 10 minutes.

6. Remove the pot from the heat, add chipotle peppers with adobo sauce and smoked cumin, and purée the soup until smooth with an immersion blender.

7. Add the heavy cream and cilantro and stir well to combine. Season to taste with additional salt and pepper.

8. Return to the stove and warm to serving temperature.

tip!

Use an ice cube tray to freeze the remaining chipotles with adobo sauce—we stick one chile and a little sauce in each divot and then transfer to a labeled airtight container or freezer bag once frozen.

molinaro's mushroom barley
with Parmesan mushroom broth

Sometimes we make things only because we love them. This soup is an example of just that. Zingerman's Delicatessen makes a fantastic beef version so we decided we'd offer a vegetarian-friendly one. The dried porcinis, three different fresh mushrooms, and two broths make for a richly flavored and supremely nourishing soup. If you leave out the Parmesan, it becomes a tasty vegan option.

Serves 6 to 8 as a main dish

Dried porcini mushrooms	1 (.75-oz) pkg	
Olive oil, divided	¼ cup	50 grams
Shiitake mushrooms, ½-dice	2¼ cups	141 grams
Oyster mushrooms, ½-dice	2¼ cups	141 grams
Crimini mushrooms, ½-dice	2¼ cups	141 grams
Fine sea salt & ground black pepper		
Fresh thyme	8 to 10 sprigs	5 grams
Garlic, minced	2 cloves	14 grams
Celery, ½-inch dice	1 cup	141 grams
Carrot, ½-inch dice	1 cup	141 grams
Yellow onion, ½-inch dice	1 cup	141 grams
All-purpose flour	2 tablespoons	23 grams
Parmesan mushroom broth (see recipe that follows)	3 cups	680 grams
Vegetable broth	8 cups	1896 grams
Pearled barley, soaked overnight and drained	1 cup	227 grams
Parsley, finely chopped	¼ cup	5 grams
Red wine vinegar	1 tablespoon	18 grams

1. Make parmesan mushroom broth (see recipe that follows).

2. In a small bowl, place the dried porcini mushrooms and cover with 1 cup of boiling water. Allow the mushrooms to steep for 15 minutes, then remove them, reserving the steeping liquid, and roughly chop the mushrooms.

3. In a large stockpot, heat 2 tablespoons of the oil over medium heat until shimmering, then add the shiitake, oyster, crimini mushrooms, and a generous sprinkle of salt, and sauté until slightly caramelized, 10 to 15 minutes. Remove them from the pot and reserve them in a bowl.

4. In the stockpot, still over medium heat, add the remaining 2 tablespoons of oil, the celery, carrots, onion, and thyme and sauté until onions have started to soften and become translucent, about 10 minutes. Add the minced garlic and sauté for 1 more minute.

5. Add the cooked mushrooms and chopped porcini mushrooms to the stockpot and sprinkle the flour over all of the vegetables, stirring once or twice to incorporate.

6. Add the Parmesan mushroom broth, vegetable broth, and reserved mushroom steeping liquid to the stockpot. When adding the latter, pour in slowly, in order to not disturb the gritty sediment at the bottom of the bowl.

7. Add the pearled barley and bring the soup to a boil over medium-high heat, then reduce heat to medium to medium-low and simmer, covered, until the soup has reduced slightly and the barley is tender, 30 to 45 minutes.

8. Stir in the parsley and red wine vinegar, then season to taste with salt and pepper.

continued on following page >

bread pairing
This soup pairs wonderfully with toasted slices of our Parmesan Pepper bread.

parmesan mushroom broth

Makes about 3 cups of broth

Olive oil	1 tablespoon	14 grams
Cremini mushrooms, quartered	2 cups	159 grams
Leek tops, roughly chopped	3 or 4 leaves	27 grams
Yellow onion, roughly chopped	½ of a small onion	60 grams
Garlic, crushed	6 cloves	50 grams
Fresh parsley	3 or 4 sprigs	8 grams
Black peppercorns	½ teaspoon	1 gram
Parmesan rinds	2 cups	431 grams
Bay leaf	1	

1. In a medium stockpot, heat the oil over medium heat until shimmering, then add the mushrooms, leek tops, and onion, and sauté until onions begins to soften and become translucent, about 10 minutes. Add the garlic and sauté for another minute or two.

2. Add the parsley, peppercorns, Parmesan rinds, bay leaf, and 4 cups of water and simmer, covered, for about an hour. Stir occasionally to prevent Parmesan rinds from sticking to the bottom of the pot.

3. Strain stock and reserve. Discard ingredients, they've given all they can. (Or nibble on the mushrooms as cook's treats, we won't tell!)

tip!

If you don't have a scale, it can be hard to measure Parmesan rinds. Aim for four large pieces, each about 4-by-4 inches.

sarah molinaro

Who is Molinaro you ask?

Why she's Sara Molinaro, the fearless leader of BAKE!, our hands-on baking school. She's been with us for a few years now and we wanted to honor her contributions to our work by naming something we make after her. Alliteration and Sara's Italian heritage made this soup a perfect choice.

Sara's Path to the Bakehouse

In 2017, in a piece on our Bakehouse blog, "Not a Lady of Leisure," Sara shared with us her fascinating path to the Bakehouse. Her resume reads like an adventurous travel log. Summers cooking and baking at a family owned lodge in Alaska's Denali National Park. Feeding fracking workers at "Man Camps" in North Dakota and Texas. Cooking Indian dishes as a personal chef to an Indian family in New York. Making pastries at Cambridge University in England. Catering swanky parties at the Ritz Carlton, then running a homeless shelter kitchen, both in San Francisco. She also lived in China for a year, but did not work at all during that time. "I am not good at being a lady of leisure, so I came home," she says.

It's probably no surprise, then, amidst her travels, that Sara picked up, not one, but three degrees along the way, all while working and experiencing life through food. She earned a Culinary Arts Associate's Degree in Baking, a Bachelor's Degree in Psychology, and a Masters of Management and Hospitality from Cornell.

So how did Sara's adventures land her in Ann Arbor? Growing up in Chicago, her mom was a foodie and so she knew of Zingerman's. Later in life, Sara's best friend lived in Ann Arbor and they went to Zingerman's Delicatessen together on visits. "I've been a Zingerman's fan for a long time. I shipped myself cosmic cakes in China."

So, naturally when Sara saw the job opening for the BAKE! Principal at Zingerman's Bakehouse she jumped on it. But how did she know it was the right job for her, and worthy of moving from New York for, besides her love of cosmic cakes? "I knew enough about the company and how employees and customers were treated. I liked those values and wanted to be in that kind of organization. The good food and good ingredients here were key too, of course."

Today, Sara spearheads our hands-on baking school; teaching classes, developing recipes, leading the other instructors and staff, and coordinating private baking classes. She describes her approach to teaching like this "When I'm teaching I want it to seem accessible and not judgemental or arrogant, otherwise people won't learn. We all make mistakes. I like to share the time I burned something and stories like that. It puts them at ease. I got here from making mistakes and learning along the way."

moroccan harira

Traditional full-flavored foods are our expertise at Zingerman's and Moroccan Harira is a perfectly fitting example. It's considered the national soup of Morocco, is made in most homes and served in many restaurants. The combination of green lentils, chickpeas, spices, and vegetables makes it a meal in a bowl. Dial up the amount of harissa if you'd like a little more of a kick.

Serves 6 to 8 as a main dish

Olive oil	3 tablespoons	40 grams
Yellow onion, ½-inch dice	2 cups	304 grams
Celery, ½-inch dice	1 cup	127 grams
Carrot, ½-inch dice	4 cups	576 grams
Fine sea salt & ground black pepper		
Ground turmeric	½ teaspoon	3 grams
Ground cumin	1 teaspoon	2 grams
Harissa	1 tablespoon	14 grams
Crushed tomatoes	1 (14.5-oz) can	
Vegetable stock	10 cups	2370 grams
Fresh parsley, leaves finely chopped	1 bunch	77 grams
Fresh cilantro, leaves finely chopped	1 bunch	77 grams
Dried chickpeas, soaked overnight	1 cup	200 grams
Green lentils	1 cup	200 grams
All-purpose flour	2 tablespoons	18 grams
Egg	1	
Fresh lemon juice	¼ cup	59 grams

bread pairing

We enjoy this soup with toasted Sesame Semolina bread, brushed with olive oil and rubbed with a little garlic.

1. In a large stockpot, heat the oil over medium heat until shimmering, then add the onion, celery, carrots, and a generous sprinkle of salt and pepper. Sauté the vegetables until just slightly tender, about 10 minutes.

2. Add the turmeric, cumin, harissa, crushed tomatoes, stock, and ¾ of the herbs, reserving ¼ for garnish. Bring to a boil over medium-high heat, then reduce heat to medium-low and simmer uncovered for 25 minutes.

3. Drain the chickpeas, add them to the soup, and simmer, uncovered, until almost tender, about 20 minutes.

4. Add the lentils and simmer, uncovered, until tender, 15 to 20 minutes. By this point, the liquid in the stockpot will have reduced a fair amount—that's to be expected.

5. In a medium bowl, whisk together flour, egg, lemon juice, and 2 cups of water. Stir this mixture into the soup and simmer until the soup has thickened, 5 minutes.

6. Taste the soup and season as needed with additional salt and pepper.

7. Warm to serving temperature and garnish with parsley and cilantro.

harira—a star of moroccan cuisine

A key mercantile hub along ancient trade routes, Morocco developed a cuisine ripe with Arabic, African, French, Mediterranean, and Middle Eastern influences. It's this blending of cultures and ideas, together with a penchant for dried fruits, such as dates and figs, preserved lemons, nuts, and the blending of fresh herbs and spices, that give Moroccan food its unique character and distinctive and delicious taste. Harira, Morrocco's national soup, is traditionally served to break the fast at sunset, during the month-long Muslim observance of Ramadan and is often accompanied by a lemon slice and crusty bread, a small bowl of lemon juice for added punch, and a plate of figs.

persian chicken stew
with chicken stock

Our Persian Chicken Stew gets its name from the combination of dried Persian limes (also known as "Limu Omani") and dried fenugreek leaves (also known as "Kasuri Methi") we add to give the stew a distinctive Middle Eastern flavor. The dried limes, which are boiled briefly in salt brine, and then laid out in the sun to dry out and darken over the course of several weeks, are an essential ingredient in the soups and stews of Iran (formerly known as Persia), Iraq, Israel, and the Gulf States. In this stew, the limes impart a tangy aromatic citrus note that's complemented by a deep layer of earthy muskiness reminiscent of fermentation. Fenugreek leaves are another culinary staple in Middle Eastern cooking. As an aromatic in soups and stews, their taste is similar to a combination of celery and fennel with a slightly bitter bite.

Serves 6 to 8 as a main dish

Vegetable oil, or other neutral-flavored oil	¼ cup	58 grams
Chicken thighs, boneless and skinless, 1-inch cubes	1 (2-lb) pkg	
Fine sea salt & ground black pepper		
Yellow onion, ½-inch dice	2 cups	308 grams
Ground turmeric	2 tablespoons	9 grams
Dried fenugreek leaves	¼ cup	4 grams
Scallions, thinly sliced	3 bunches	323 grams
Fresh parsley, leaves finely chopped	1 bunch	63 grams
Fresh cilantro, leaves finely chopped	½ bunch	36 grams
Chicken stock (see recipe that follows)	10 cups	2370 grams
Dried Persian limes	7 whole limes	36 grams
Red kidney beans	2 (15-oz) cans	

bread pairing This stew pairs nicely with a slice of toasted Sesame Semolina bread or a big chunk of our Paesano loaf.

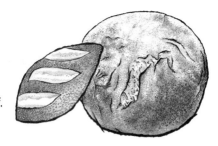

1. Make chicken stock (see recipe that follows).

2. In a large stockpot, heat the oil over medium-high heat until shimmering, then carefully add the thighs, and a generous sprinkle of salt and pepper, and sauté until chicken is no longer pink, 5 to 10 minutes.

3. Reduce the heat to medium, add the onions, turmeric, and fenugreek leaves to the pot, and sauté until onions are tender and translucent, stirring often, 10 to 15 minutes.

4. Stir in the scallions, parsley, and cilantro, and sauté until wilted and dark green, about 5 minutes.

5. Add the stock and limes (limes will float on top of stew), bring stew to a boil over medium heat, then reduce heat to medium-low and let simmer for 20 minutes.

6. Using tongs and a paring knife, pierce the limes and submerge them in the stew. Simmer an additional 20 minutes on low heat.

7. Add the kidney beans and heat through. Season to taste with additional salt and pepper.

tip!

Dried whole Persian limes and dried fenugreek leaves are available at Middle Eastern specialty grocery stores and also online at such sites as Kalustyans.com

continued on following page >

chicken stock

Each week, the Bakehouse's savory kitchen roasts nearly 50 whole chickens, with little going to waste: the meat goes into our tasty chicken salad and chicken noodle soup, leaving all those leftover bones and carcasses for chicken stock. The savory kitchen uses the traditional low and slow method of simmering a large quantity of bones in water, along with vegetables and aromatics, for several hours. For home cooks short on time and leftover chicken bones, the following recipe is a good alternative. Using (most of) a whole chicken and browning the meat and bones results in a rich and flavorful chicken stock in a fraction of the time—less than 2 hours.

Makes about 10 cups

Whole chicken	4 lbs	
Vegetable oil	2 tablespoons	9 grams
Fine sea salt, split	2 teaspoons	12 grams
Ground black pepper, split	2 teaspoons	5 grams
Yellow onion, 1-inch dice	1 large	250 grams
Carrot, 2-inch pieces	2 large	292 grams
Celery, 2-inch pieces	2 large	140 grams
Fresh parsley	½ small bunch	30 grams
Fresh thyme	5 sprigs	3 grams
Garlic, smashed	2 cloves	16 grams
Black peppercorns	8	
Bay leaves	2	

1. Cut chicken into 9 pieces: 2 thighs, 2 drumsticks, 2 wings, 2 breast filets, and 1 back. Then, cut thighs, drumsticks, wings, back, and remaining carcass into 2-inch pieces; save the 2 breast filets for another use. Season chicken pieces with half of the salt and pepper.

2. Heat oil in a large stockpot over medium-high heat until shimmering. Add half of the chicken pieces to the pot (avoid overcrowding) and sauté until lightly brown on all sides, about 5 minutes; transfer to a large bowl. Repeat with remaining chicken pieces using fat left in the pot, and transfer to the bowl.

3. Add onion to the fat left in the pot and sauté until starting to soften, about 5 minutes. Return browned chicken pieces and any accumulated juices to pot, add carrots, celery, garlic, parsley, and thyme and season mixture with remaining salt and pepper. Cover pot, and reduce heat to low. Cook, stirring occasionally, until chicken has released its juices, 20 to 30 minutes.

4. Add 12 cups of water, peppercorns, and bay leaves and bring to a boil. Cover, reduce to a gentle simmer, and cook, skimming as needed, until stock tastes rich and flavorful, about 30 minutes longer.

5. Remove large bones and solids from the pot with a slotted spoon or spider strainer, then strain the stock through a fine mesh sieve. Let stock settle for 5 to 10 minutes, then remove the fat using a wide, shallow spoon or fat separator. If time and space permits, allow stock to come to room temperature and then cool in the refrigerator. As it cools, additional fat will harden into a solid layer that can be easily lifted off with a spoon. If you want to remove any lingering sediment from the vegetables and aromatics, strain the stock a second time through a fine mesh sieve lined with cheesecloth.

sri Lankan LentiL

Sri Lankan Lentil gets its name from the Sri Lankan White Curry spice blend we use from Canadian spice importers, Épices de Cru. They sell their spices whole, to maintain flavor and freshness, and this blend is a mild mix with notes of cinnamon, lemongrass, and tropical herbs. It's called a white curry both because it doesn't contain red chiles or turmeric and it's usually paired with coconut milk, as we do in this warming, vegan soup.

Makes 6 to 8 main dish servings

Red lentils	2⅓ cups	508 grams
Fresh ginger, minced	3 tablespoons	50 grams
Garlic, minced	2 or 3 cloves	18 grams
Carrots, ½-inch dice	2 cups	304 grams
Yellow onions, ½-inch dice	2 cups	304 grams
Bay leaves	3	
Ground Sri Lankan white curry	2 tablespoons	14 grams
Crushed tomatoes	1 (15-oz) can	
Coconut milk	2 (13.5-oz) cans	
Fresh cilantro, finely chopped	⅓ cup	18 grams
Fine sea salt & ground black pepper		

1. Sort through the lentils to ensure there are no stones or dirt clumps.

2. Add lentils to a large stockpot over medium-high heat, along with 6½ cups of water, and bring to a boil.

3. Add the ginger, garlic, carrots, yellow onions, bay leaves, ground curry, crushed tomatoes, and coconut milk. Reduce to a simmer and cook until lentils, carrots, and onions are tender, 30 to 40 minutes, stirring occasionally to reduce sticking.

4. Remove from heat, stir in cilantro and season to taste with salt and pepper.

bread pairing

Try serving over our Ruby's Cubes (olive oil-tossed croutons dusted with a little salt and pepper) to give it a little extra body.

tomato de-vine

Our collection of soup recipes wouldn't be complete without our creamy Tomato De-Vine—it's a staple of Grilled Cheese Wednesdays at the Bakehouse. Enjoy this smooth and mellow version of an American classic—easy to make and loved by many.

Serves 6 to 8 as a main dish

Crushed tomatoes	3 (28-oz) + 1 (14.5-oz) cans	
Granulated sugar	Scant ⅓ cup	57 grams
Butter	16 tablespoons	227 grams
Yellow onion, ½-inch dice	1 cup	150 grams
All-purpose flour	1⅓ cups	191 grams
Whole milk	4½ cups	1103 grams
Fine sea salt	3 teaspoons	18 grams
Ground black pepper	2 teaspoons	5 grams

1. In a large stockpot, combine all 4 cans of tomatoes and sugar. Warm on low heat until hot. Stir frequently to make sure it does not burn.

2. In a medium pot, over medium heat, add the butter and onions, and sauté onions until tender and translucent, 10 to 15 minutes.

3. Add the flour to the onions and stir constantly until the mixture is a light brown color, resembling peanut butter, 3 to 5 minutes.

4. Increase the heat to medium-high and, while whisking constantly, slowly add the milk to the onion and flour mixture to make a thick béchamel sauce.

5. Remove the large stockpot from heat, add in the béchamel, salt, and pepper, and purée the soup until smooth with an immersion blender.

6. Return to the heat and warm to serving temperature.

Enjoy this classic soup like we do at the Bakehouse: with grilled cheese made on either our State St. Wheat or Better Than San Francisco Sourdough.

grilled cheese wednesday

Nearly every week someone asks us to add a menu item as a restaurant might, not really considering what a bakery can do in an 800-square-foot retail shop. Some years ago in a weak moment, we agreed to buy a press grill and make grilled cheese sandwiches to sell each Wednesday at lunch time, paired with our creamy Tomato De-Vine soup. We felt we were staffed to do it and that the shop could pull it off.

Well, from the start the sandwiches were a success, and we were consistently selling all that we had prepared by 1 pm every Wednesday afternoon. Our sales went from 20 a day to 30 to 40 and on and on. After a couple of years, the demand outgrew our ability to grill the sandwiches on two press grills in the Bakehouse so we moved the operation over to the 12-burner stove in our front classroom at BAKE!

Our guests would order their sandwiches in the shop and then walk across the courtyard to the classroom to pick them up. Now, with a fully equipped savory kitchen, our grilled cheese sandwich making has returned to the Bakehouse and guests can now order and pick up their sandwiches in the shop. Made with our Better than San Francisco Sourdough bread, New York Cheddar cheese, and if you'd like, honey mustard and tomatoes ("The Works"), the sandwiches, paired with our Tomato De-Vine soup, make many people happy each Wednesday. Nowadays, we make upward of 200 sandwiches. It's definitely a comforting and tasty lunch to look forward to every week. Wednesdays will always mean grilled cheese with Tomato De-Vine soup at the Bakehouse.

turkey urfa chili

As you might guess, this chili is made with ground turkey meat. But its name also comes from an important ingredient—particularly flavorful red-black pepper flakes from the region of Urfa in Turkey. It's a testament to how the choice of particular ingredients can make a noticeable difference in a simple recipe.

Do as our customers do and make both this chili and our 5 O'Clock Cheddar Ale at the same time and have your dining mates mix them together. People swear by the combination, the actual proportions are a personal choice.

Serves 6 to 8 as a main dish

Canola oil	2 tablespoons	23 grams
Onions, ½-inch dice	1¼ cups	171 grams
Fine sea salt		
Garlic, minced	3 cloves	25 grams
Ground turkey	1 (1-lb) pkg	
Cumin	2½ teaspoons	5 grams
Green chili powder	2½ teaspoons	5 grams
Urfa pepper flakes	1½ tablespoons	13 grams
Ground black pepper	1 teaspoon	2 grams
Diced tomatoes	1 (28-oz) can	
Crushed tomatoes	1 (28-oz) can	
Kidney beans	3 (15-oz) cans	
Sour cream for topping (optional)		
Scallions, sliced, for topping (optional)		

1. In a large stockpot over medium heat, add the oil and heat until shimmering, then add the onions and a generous sprinkle of salt, and sauté until tender and translucent, 10 to 15 minutes.

2. Add the ground turkey and the minced garlic. Cook, stirring frequently, until turkey is completely cooked, about 5 minutes, actively breaking up the turkey as you stir to avoid clumping.

3. Add the cumin, green chili powder, Urfa pepper, and black pepper. Stir to incorporate the spices and cook for 3 minutes.

4. Add the beans and both kinds of tomatoes. Mix well. Bring to a simmer and cook for 30 minutes, stirring frequently to avoid scorching. Garnish with sour cream and scallions if desired.

bread pairing

Personally, we like this chili with a chunk of Better Than San Francisco Sourdough bread.

thursday is tipsy turkey day!

We've been serving up our 5 O'clock Cheddar Ale (see recipe on pages 16–17) and Mary Kalinowski's Turkey Urfa Chili in the Bakeshop on Thursdays for as long as we can remember. When we first paired them up, they seemed like dissimilar soups that would give folks a tasty choice of two distinctive flavors. We never imagined that a shop guest would ask us to mix the two, serving up a combined bowl of Cheddar Ale and Turkey Chili. The discovery was genius and the Bakeshop manager at the time, Jake Blachowicz,

gave the unusual yet flavorful combo the catchy name of *Tipsy Turkey*! (Get it?—Tipsy/Cheddar Ale; Turkey/Turkey Chili.) Now a Thursday standard and fan favorite, shop guests clamor for one of the most eclectic concoctions we've ever experienced in our almost three decades in the food business. Some like the ratio of half and half, others prefer topping their chili with a bit of Cheddar Ale or vice versa. Any way you serve it up, the combination makes for one tasty bowl of hot chili!

Vichyssoise

Vichyssoise is a chilled potato leek soup that was created by the French chef, Louis Diat in 1917. He served it at New York's Ritz Carlton to help his customers cool off in the heat of the summer and now we do the same to help our Bakeshop guests beat the heat as well. Swap in vegetable broth to make it vegetarian-friendly, and if you'd like to serve it hot instead, consider not fully puréeing it, so that it maintains some texture from the potatoes.

Makes 8 to 10 appetizer servings

Olive oil	⅓ cup	90 grams
Leeks	2	453 grams
Fine sea salt & ground black pepper		
Russet potatoes, peeled, ½-inch dice	2 large	453 grams
Chicken broth	4 cups	453 grams
Heavy cream	4 cups	924 grams
Ground nutmeg	2 teaspoons	5 grams
Minced chives or thinly sliced scallions for garnish		

This soup is delicious accompanied with some of our Pecan Raisin bread crisps, full-flavored cheese, and summer berries.

1. To prepare the leeks, remove the roots and dark green top so that you are left with the white and very lightest green parts of the stalk. Save the green top and roots for stock or another use. Rinse the exterior and then cut the base in half and rinse again to remove any interior dirt. Slice into ½-inch thick half-moons. Place a colander in a bowl, fill with cold water, then submerge leek pieces and swish around to dislodge any grit between the layers. Allow the leeks to sit for a minute or two to allow the grit to settle to the bottom of the bowl, then gently lift out the colander and discard the rinse water.

2. In a large stockpot, heat the oil over medium heat until shimmering. Add the leeks and season with salt and pepper. Sauté until soft and translucent, turning down heat as needed to make sure they do not take on any color, 5 to 10 minutes.

3. Add the potatoes and broth and bring to a boil over medium-high heat, reduce to a simmer and cook until potatoes are very soft, 30 to 40 minutes.

4. Add the cream, nutmeg, and pepper and purée with an immersion blender until very smooth. Taste and adjust seasoning.

5. Served chilled, garnished with minced chives or scallions.

tip!

Don't stick the hot stockpot full of soup directly into the fridge! This can raise the temperature inside the fridge, which could put your other food at risk.

To help it cool down safely, either make an ice bath in your (clean) sink with cold water and ice, then place the pot in the ice bath (making sure the water doesn't mix into the soup). Or, transfer the soup to smaller containers and allow them to cool on the counter to room temperature before covering and transferring into the fridge.

west african peanut stew

This was one of our original soups from Mary Kalinowski, and it was a customer favorite for many years. The Bakehouse, and BAKE!, our hands-on baking school, are now peanut-free, so we no longer sell it in our shop or teach it, but it's still a flavorful favorite that we like to make at home. It's a rich and complex soup that we recommend serving with a cooling side salad of crisp vegetables. A fitting dessert to round it out would be chilled tropical fruits like mango, kiwi, and pineapple.

Serves 6 to 8 as a main dish

Canola oil	2 tablespoons	28 grams
Yellow onion, ½-inch dice	1¼ cups	170 grams
Celery, ½-inch dice	1⅓ cups	170 grams
Carrots, ½-inch dice	1 cup	142 grams
Fine sea salt & ground black pepper		
Minced ginger	1 tablespoon	14 grams
Diced tomatoes	1 (14.5-oz) can	
Ground garam masala	1½ teaspoons	5 grams
Sweet potato, peeled, ½-inch dice	1 medium	476 grams
Vegetable stock	5 cups	1134 grams
Smooth peanut butter (natural, no salt added)	1¼ cups	295 grams
Muscovado sugar	2 tablespoons	28 grams
Marash pepper flakes	1 teaspoon	2 grams

bread pairing

Try pairing this curried soup with our Indian Rétes, a savory strudel of sautéed vegetables and Indian spices we make fresh daily at the Bakehouse.

1. In a large stockpot, heat the oil over medium heat until shimmering, then add the onion, celery, carrots and a generous sprinkle of salt and pepper, and sauté until onions are translucent and soft, about 10 minutes.

2. Add ginger and sauté for an additional 5 minutes.

3. Add diced tomatoes and garam masala and cook for 5 more minutes.

4. Add the sweet potatoes and stock, bring to a boil over medium-high heat, then lower to a simmer and continue cooking until the potatoes are cooked through, about 20 minutes.

5. Add the peanut butter, sugar, and Marash pepper and purée the soup until smooth with an immersion blender.

6. Season to taste with salt and pepper. Warm to serving temperature and serve.

tip!

We're big fans of muscovado brown sugar. Look for brown sugar that is specifically labeled "muscovado."

Organic brown sugar is not muscovado. Muscovado is cane sugar that is refined less than white sugar, leaving much of the molasses in the end product and much more flavor.

Typical American brown sugar is actually cane sugar refined to white sugar with some molasses added back. (This explains the availability of light brown sugar and dark brown sugar.)

appreciations

MOST BOOKS have an acknowledgments page, but since we end our meetings with appreciations, ours is an appreciation page. Here are our heartfelt thanks to those who helped us on our project.

Bakeshop lunch customers, this cookbooklet is due to your regular midday support and love of our rotating soup schedule—we hope some of your favorites made the cut.

Mary Kalinowski, a former Bakehouse bread baker who opened her own soup shop and then returned to the bakery to make soups with us. Many thanks for getting us going with soup-er soups so many years ago.

Frank Carollo and Hazim Tugun, who scaled down the Bakehouse recipes to volumes that made sense for home kitchens.

Our recipe testers, including Jake Emberling, Emily Hanka, Melissa Lesz, Ally Martin, Nina Plasencia (who kindly volunteered her husband, Mason Rosselot, on her behalf), Jaison & Christina Restrick, and John Rolfe-Chin, who helped us double- and triple-check that every soup tasted just right.

Current members of the savory team, Brandon Clark, John Mason, Kristin Pills, Alicia Amormino and Luke Woodworth for getting the Soup On! everyday. And many thanks to former soup makers Angie Edwards-Hamilton, Anne Good, Hyatt Middleton, and Thomas Wilson, who created or improved recipes within these pages many moons ago.

Our Creative Services team who helped us turn these recipes into a cookbooklet. Patrick Barber, who led the layout work and printing work, and Ryan Stiner and Ian Nagy, who created such fun and engaging illustrations to garnish our copy.